D1710847

Learn With Animals

In the Jungle

By Laura Ottina
Adapted by Barbara Bakowski

Illustrated by
Sebastiano Ranchetti

WEEKLY READER®
PUBLISHING

Deep in the jungle
Is where we hide,
By the trees so high
And the river wide.

2

3

I am a macaw
With a big, strong beak.
I have bright feathers
And can learn to speak.

6

I am a spider monkey.
I live in the trees.
From branch to branch
I swing through leaves.

I am a caiman
With sharp teeth and claws.
At night when I hunt,
Stay away from my jaws!

I am a hummingbird,
So tiny and light.
The nectar from flowers
I drink with delight.

I am an iguana
Who soaks up the sun.
I lie on warm rocks
Until daytime is done.

13

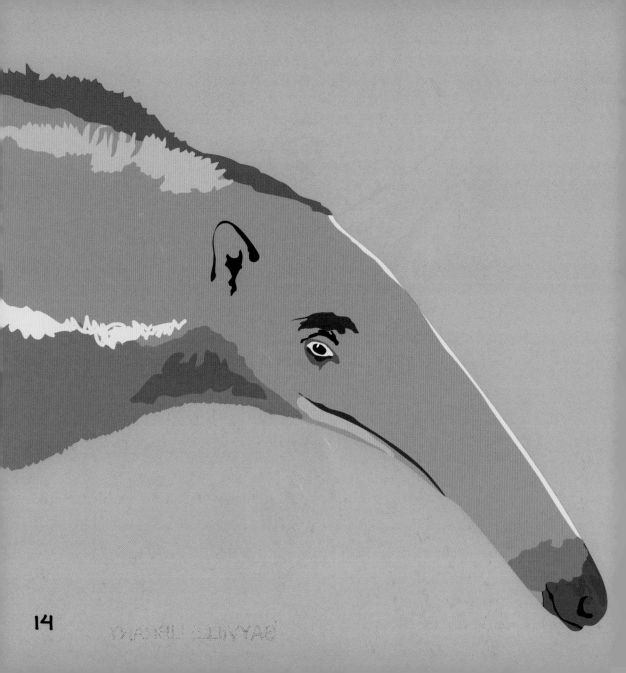

14

I am an anteater,
A hunter so tricky.
I catch bugs to eat
With my tongue so sticky.

15

I am a tree frog
With green skin so bright.
My big red eyes
Are a colorful sight.

17

18

I am a jaguar,
A cat with great speed.
My roar and big paws
Are scary indeed!

I am a toucan.
I have a long bill
With tasty fruits
And berries to fill.

I am a blue morpho,
A bright butterfly.
With beautiful wings
Through the jungle I fly.

23

Please visit our web site at www.garethstevens.com.
For a free catalog describing our list of high-quality books,
call 1-800-542-2595 (USA) or 1-800-387-3178 (Canada).
Our fax: 1-877-542-2596

Library of Congress Cataloging-in-Publication Data
Ottina, Laura.
    [Incontra gli animali nella gigungla. English]
    In the jungle / by Laura Ottina ; adapted by Barbara Bakowski ;
illustrated by Sebastiano Ranchetti.
        p. cm. — (Learn with animals)
    ISBN-10: 1-4339-1913-3   ISBN-13: 978-1-4339-1913-8 (lib. bdg.)
    ISBN-10: 1-4339-2090-5   ISBN-13: 978-1-4339-2090-5 (softcover)
    1. Jungle animals—Juvenile literature.   I. Bakowski, Barbara.   II. Ranchetti, Sebastiano, ill.
III. Title.
    QL112.088313   2010
    591.734-dc22   2008052451

This North American edition first published in 2010 by
Weekly Reader® Books
An Imprint of Gareth Stevens Publishing
1 Reader's Digest Road
Pleasantville, NY 10570-7000 USA

This U.S. edition copyright © 2010 by Gareth Stevens, Inc. International Copyright
© 2008 by Editoriale Jaca Book spa, Milan, Italy. All rights reserved. First published
in 2008 as *Incontra gli animali nella giungla* by Editoriale Jaca Book spa.

Gareth Stevens Executive Managing Editor: Lisa M. Herrington
Gareth Stevens Senior Editor: Barbara Bakowski
Gareth Stevens Creative Director: Lisa Donovan
Gareth Stevens Designer: Jennifer Ryder-Talbot

Printed in the United States of America

1 2 3 4 5 6 7 8 9 12 11 10 09

Find out more about Laura Ottina and Sebastiano Ranchetti at **www.animalsincolor.com**.